Overview

In the previous book, you learned about the basics of the Rust programming language. You got a feel for the language and even wrote your first code.

You learned how to start and build projects using Cargo and even begun a milestone project you can add to your portfolio.

Get My Rust for Backend Engineering Course!

At 20% Discount

https://masteringbackend.com/courses/rust-for-backend-engineering

This intermediate-level book dives deeper into Rust's features and concepts, enabling readers to develop more complex and robust applications.

Practical examples, exercises, and a hands-on project will ensure that you build confidence and competence in intermediate Rust programming.

Below is the table of content showing what you will learn. Let's get started.

- **Advanced-Data Structures in Rust:** Aside from data types and primary data structures, Rust supports more advanced data structures like HashMaps and Sets. Before we look into them, let's refresh our memory on the Vector data structure.

- **Advanced Methods, Enums, and Pattern Matching:** We have seen how methods work: when there is a struct, a method must be implemented for that struct to be able to use the data in the struct. Methods are also defined for enums and traits — concepts that we will explore after now. For now, let's revise some of the constructs of method implementations in general.

- **Traits and Generics in Rust:** In our earlier exploration of the *Result* and *Option* enums, you encountered using *<T, E>* and *<T>* within angle brackets. These constructs are known as generics. Generics are a powerful feature in programming that allows you to write functions, types, and structures that can work with different data types while maintaining type safety and code reusability.

- **Lifetimes in Rust:** Lifetimes are a fundamentally important concept in Rust that ensures that references remain valid and prevent issues like dangling pointers or references to memory that have been deallocated. To write safe and efficient Rust code, you must understand lifetimes and how to use them. This is one of Rust's most unique trademark features.

- **Advanced Functions and Closures:** By now, you must be good at writing functions in Rust. If you have prior programming experience, you would know that functions sometimes accept pointers as parameters. If you know functional programming, you must have heard about higher-order functions and closures. Let's take them step by step.

- **Concurrency and Multithreading in Rust:** This chapter will explore the world of concurrency and multithreading in Rust. Concurrency allows you to handle multiple tasks simultaneously, while multithreading takes advantage of multiple CPU cores for parallel execution. Rust's strong ownership and type system help ensure safe and efficient concurrent programming.

- **Concurrency and Multithreading in Rust:** This chapter will explore the world of concurrency and multithreading in Rust. Concurrency allows you to handle multiple tasks simultaneously, while multithreading takes advantage of multiple CPU cores for parallel execution. Rust's strong ownership and type system help ensure safe and efficient concurrent programming.

- **Error Handling in Rust:** In this chapter, we'll delve into Rust's intricacies of error handling. Effective error handling is a cornerstone of robust and reliable software. We'll explore the Result and Option types, learn how to use the match and ? operators for error handling, implement custom error types using the thiserror crate, and discover how the Result type aids in early returns within functions. This chapter will use real-world backend engineering scenarios to illustrate each concept.

- **File I/O and Serialization:** This comprehensive chapter will explore Rust's file input/output (I/O) operations and serialization. These topics are crucial for handling data in backend applications. We'll explore how to read and write files, perform serialization and deserialization using the serde crate, and work with various file formats like JSON and YAML. This chapter will use practical examples from a backend engineering perspective.

- **Milestone Project: Building a Task Management App:** We'll build a task management application using Rust in this exciting milestone project. This project will encompass concepts covered in the previous chapters, including structuring your code, error handling, file I/O, and more. Following these steps, you'll create a functional task manager allowing users to add, list, and mark tasks as completed.

Advanced-Data Structures in Rust

Aside from data types and primary data structures, Rust supports more advanced data structures like HashMaps and Sets. Before we look into them, let's refresh our memory on the Vector data structure.

Vectors

We defined Vectors as dynamic arrays that can grow or shrink in size. That is, elements stored in a Vector (denoted with Vec<T> in Rust, where T stands for the data type of the elements) are stored next to each other in memory. Let's see how Vectors are created in Rust. Create a new project:

```
cargo new learn_rust
```

Inside the main.rs [http://main.rs/] file, write this function by hand:

```rust
pub fn create_vector() {
    // Create a new mutable vector of type i32.
    let mut new_vector: Vec<i32> = Vec::new();
    // Print out the content of the vector.
    println!("Vector content: {:?}", new_vector);
    // Push a value into the vector.
    new_vector.push(1);
    // Print out the new content of the vector.
    println!("Vector content: {:?}", new_vector);
}
```

You should see the output:

```
Vector content: []
Vector content: [1]
```

This is how to create and update a Vector. Vectors also have these important functions that save you time:

- `.remove()` to remove an element from the Vector.

- `.get()` to access an element using its index.

- `for..in..` loop for iteration.

Note: The Vector accepts any type `T`, meaning any of these can be done in Rust:

```rust
pub fn pass_all_data_types_to_vectors() {

  // integer values.
  let numbers: Vec<i32> = vec![1,2,3,4,5];

  // floating point values.
  let temperatures: Vec<f64> = vec![36.6, 27.0, 15.3];

  // strings.
  let names: Vec<String> = vec!["Bob".to_string(), "Alice".to_string()];

  // booleans.
  let flags: Vec<bool> = vec![true, false, true, true];

  // custom structs.
  struct Person {
    name: String,
    age: u32,
  }
  let people: Vec<Person> = vec![
    Person { name: "Bob".to_string(), age: 27 },
    Person { name: "Alice".to_string(), age: 37 },
  ];
```

```rust
// enums:
  enum FilterOptions {
    Free,
    Paid,
    Bonus,
  }
  let filters: Vec<FilterOptions> = vec![FilterOptions::Free, FilterOptions::Paid, FilterOpti
ons::Bonus];
  // mixed types using trait objects.
  let mixed: Vec<Box<dyn std::fmt::Debug>> = vec![
    Box::new(42),
    Box::new("Alice".to_string()),
  ];
}
```

Now that we understand Vectors, let's explore HashMaps.

HashMaps

HashMaps in Rust are similar to Maps or HashMaps in another programming language. They are used to map keys of any type to values of any type. Let's see how to create and populate a HashMap:

```rust
// Import collections package from STD.
use std::collections::HashMap;

pub fn create_hashmap() {
    // Create a new hashmap.
    let mut data = HashMap::new();
    // Insert data into this hashmap.
    data.insert(String::from("One"), 1);
    data.insert(String::from("Two"), 2);
    // Check the content of the hashmap.
    println!("Content of data: {:?}", data);
}
```

Next, let's see how to access a value in the HashMap or return a message if the value is not found:

```rust
// Accessing value in the HashMap.
if let Some(data) = data.get("One") {
    println!("The first data here is: {}", data);
} else {
    // Handling Nonexistent keys.
    println!("That data is not found.");
}
```

Finally, let's see how to iterate over the values in the HashMap and how to remove values from it:

```rust
// Iterating over the HashMap.
for (key, data) in &data {
    println!("{} matches with {}", key, data);
}

// Remove values form the HashMap.
data.remove("Two");
println!("Content of data: {:?}", data);
```

In several software systems, HashMaps are often used in the following scenarios:

1. In implementing caching mechanisms, quick lookups will reduce resource-intensive operations like database queries or expensive calculations.

2. In user session management, store session information like user IDs, session tokens, etc., and quickly find an account using a credential such as email.

3. In data indexing and searching operations popular in search engines of different systems.

4. Managing resources like database connections, threads, network sockets, etc., is important in resource pools.

5. Others.

Note: If you want to quickly simulate a database but don't want to go through the stress of setting up one, you can quickly simulate one in your code using a HashMap, as you have seen. In the next section, you will see an example of this.

Great! Now that we have learned about Collections in Rust let's move on to more important concepts: Methods and Enumerations.

Exercises

1. Vectors and HashMaps: Write a program that stores user input in a vector. Implement a function that finds the frequency of each unique element in the vector and displays the results using a HashMap.

2. Iteration Patterns: Create a custom struct containing information about books (title, author, genre, etc.). Store multiple instances of this struct in a vector. Use iteration patterns to filter and display specific books based on certain criteria.

Advanced Methods, Enums, and Pattern Matching

We have seen how methods work: when there is a struct, a method must be implemented for that struct to be able to use the data in the struct.

Methods are also defined for enums and traits — concepts that we will explore after now. For now, let's revise some of the constructs of method implementations in general.

We will build a simple user session management program using everything we have learned. Create a new project called `session_mgt` using Cargo.

Create a module called `methods.rs` and export it to the `main.rs` file. If you don't know how to do this, read the Beginner Rust book [https://masteringbackend.com/books/rust-essentials].

Next, type this code in the `methods.rs` file by yourself, trying to understand what is happening:

```rust
use rand::Rng;

// Create the underlying struct for the User.
#[derive(Debug, Clone)]
pub struct User {
    pub id: u32,
    pub username: String,
    pub email: String,
}

// Implement the User struct.
impl User {
    // new is a constructor function for User that creates a new user.
    pub fn new(id: u32, username: &str, email: &str) -> Self {
        User {
            id,
            username: username.to_string(),
            email: email.to_string() }
    }
}

// Create the underlying struct for the Session.
#[derive(Debug, Clone)]
pub struct Session {
    pub user_id: u32,
    pub token: String,
}
```

```rust
// Implement the Session struct {
impl Session {
    // new is a constructor function for Session that creates a new user session.
    pub fn new(user_id: u32) -> Self {
        let token = rand::thread_rng()
        .sample_iter(rand::distributions::Alphanumeric)
        .take(16)
        .map(char::from)
        .collect();

    Session { user_id, token }
    }
}
```

Great! We successfully created two structs: User and Senior . Notice how we used the pub keyword to judiciously export the struct's properties, the struct itself, and the functions that implement it.

If you come from a functional programming language that uses structs, you will not be new to method implementations for structs. When creating a new struct, it is ideal to always have a constructor function using the new function name. This name is not compulsory but has become conventional practice.

> **Note:** When writing code, keep in mind that the code is not being read by the user of the software, but by another programmer like you. Hence, optimize the code for good developer experience, and the software for good user experience.

Another observation from the code above is the use of the self keyword. This is common with other functional languages. By rule of thumb, the new constructor function always returns an instance of the struct (called self). Other functions look somewhat like this below. Inside the impl User block, add this:

```rust
// Function to get a user by ID from the simulated user database.
pub fn get_user_by_id(user_id: u32, user_db: &HashMap<u32, User>) -> Option<&User> {
    user_db.get(&user_id)
}

// Function to update a user's credential in the user database.
pub fn update_user_credential(user_id: u32, new_username: &str, new_email: &str, user_db: &mut HashMap<u32, User>) -> bool {
    if let Some(user) = user_db.get_mut(&user_id) {
        user.username = new_username.to_string();
        user.email = new_email.to_string();
        true
    } else {
        false
    }
}

// Method to display the details of current user instance.
pub fn display_user_details(&self){
    println!("ID: {}, Username: {}, Email: {}", self.id, self.username, self.email);
}
```

The methods above are the common CRUD operations peculiar to backend systems. If you observe, you will notice that the display_user_details takes a &user parameter, while others do not. Methods can take self, &self, &mut self, or no self parameter.

- self indicates that the method takes ownership of the instance and can modify it.

- &self indicates that the method borrows the instance immutably, allowing read-only access.

- &mut self indicates that the method borrows the instance mutably, allowing read-write access.

- No self parameter means the method doesn't require access to the instance's data.

Note: If the if let Some control method looks alien to you. You will learn about it under Pattern Matching in this section.

Enums and complex data representations

Enums, short for enumerations, are a powerful Rust feature that allows you to define a custom type representing a set of distinct values. It is used to create types with a fixed set of possible values, meaning you can use them to represent different states, options, or variants. Let's see how to define enums.

Defining Enums

Use the `enum` keyword to define an enum:

```
enum HTTPStatus {
    Ok,
    NotFound,
    BadRequest,
    InternalServerError
    // etc.
}
```

Enums also take the `pub` keyword when used in a module. The properties in an Enum can have specified data types:

```
pub enum ApiResponse {
    Success(String),
    Error(String),
}
```

This is pretty much all you need to know about enums. Let's explore how to use enumerated data representations by pattern matching.

Pattern matching with Enums

Pattern matching with enums is essential for handling different outcomes in software systems. Let's see how this works from our previous enum example:

18

```rust
fn process_response(response: ApiResponse) {
  match response {
    ApiResponse::Success(msg) => {
      println!("Success: {}", msg);
    }
    ApiResponse::Error(msg) => {
      println!("Error: {}", msg)
    }
  }
}
```

Complex data representation

Enums can hold more complex data, useful for representing structured information. Let's see an example:

```rust
pub enum Request {
  Get(String),
  Post { path: String, body: String },
}
```

Enums and Result in error handling

We are yet to see how Error handling works in Rust, but here is just a peek at how Enums are used in handling errors:

```
pub enum Result<T, E> {
  Ok(T),
  Err(E),
}
```

Enums and Option for detecting presence and absence.

Like the Result enum, the Option enum is another fundamental construct in Rust that plays a crucial role in handling nullable values and representing the presence or absence of a value. Let's explore the Option enum and its relevance in backend engineering.

The Option Enum

The Option enum is defined in Rust's standard library and represents the presence or absence of a value. It is commonly used to handle cases where a value might be missing or is optional. The Option enum has two variants: Some (indicating the presence of a value) and None (indicating the absence of a value).

Here's the definition of the Option enum:

```
enum Option<T> {
  Some(T),
  None,
}
```

Using Option in real-world systems

In a real-world context, the Option enum is extremely valuable for handling nullable values, representing optional data, and indicating the absence of certain information. Here are some scenarios where Option is commonly used:

1. User Authentication:

When handling user authentication, you might need to represent the absence of an authenticated user.

```
fn authenticate_user(username: &str, password: &str) -> Option<User> {
    // Authenticate the user and return Some(User) if successful, None otherwise
}
```

1. Database Queries:

When querying a database, certain rows might not exist.

```
fn get_user_by_id(id: u32) -> Option<User> {
    // Retrieve user from the database; return Some(User) if found, None otherwise
}
```

We did this in our session management application under HashMaps above.

1. Optional Configuration:

Backend systems often have optional configuration settings.

```
fn read_config(key: &cstr) -> Option<String> {
    // Read configuration value; return Some(value) if present, None otherwise
}
```

Pattern Matching with Option

Pattern matching with the Option enum is a crucial technique to extract or handle the absence of values. Here's an example:

```
fn main() {
    let maybe_value: Option<i32> = Some(42);

    match maybe_value {
        Some(value) => {
            println!("Got a value: {}", value);
        }
        None => {
            println!("No value found.");
        }
    }
}
```

Using Option and Result Together

Option and Result are often used together for comprehensive error handling. While Result indicates success or failure along with an error message, Option indicates the presence or absence of a value.

```
fn find_user_by_id(id: u32) -> Result<Option<User>, String> {
    // Search for the user by ID
    // Return Ok(Some(User)) if found, Ok(None) if not found, Err(error) if error occurs
}
```

The Option enum is a core construct in Rust that is vital for handling nullable values and representing optional data. In backend engineering, it helps manage cases where values might be missing or optional, enabling more precise and safer handling of data and outcomes.

The if let Some control flow

The if let Some control flow construct in Rust is a convenient way to handle pattern matching, specifically when you're interested in handling cases where an Option holds a Some variant. This is particularly useful when you want to extract and work with the value contained within a Some variant of an Option without having to explicitly match all possible variants of the Option.

The basic syntax of the if let Some construct is as follows:

```
if let Some(pattern) = some_option {
    // Code to execute if the option contains a Some value
}
```

- pattern : A pattern that matches the value inside the Some variant.

- some_option : The Option you want to match against.

Example

Let's look at a simple example to illustrate how if let Some works:

```
fn main() {
  let maybe_number: Option<i32> = Some(42);

  if let Some(number) = maybe_number {
    println!("Got a number: {}", number);
  } else {
    println!("No number found.");
  }
}
```

In this example, if maybe_number contains a Some variant with a value, the value will be bound to the variable number, and the code inside the block will execute. If maybe_number is a None variant, the else block will execute.

Benefits of if let Some

1. Conciseness: It provides a more concise way to handle a specific case without explicitly handling all cases of an Option.

2. Readability: It makes the code more readable by avoiding the need for a full match expression when you are only interested in one specific variant.

Nested if let Some

You can use nested if let Some constructs to handle more complex situations where multiple Option values need to be checked.

```rust
fn main() {
    let maybe_number1: Option<i32> = Some(42);
    let maybe_number2: Option<i32> = Some(99);

    if let Some(number1) = maybe_number1 {
        if let Some(number2) = maybe_number2 {
            println!("Got numbers: {} and {}", number1, number2);
        } else {
            println!("No number2 found.");
        }
    } else {
        println!("No number1 found.");
    }
}
```

Caveats

- While if let Some is convenient for handling the Some variant, it doesn't provide a way to handle the None variant. Using a match expression is more appropriate if you need to handle both Some and None.

- Using a match expression is recommended if you need to perform more complex patterns or multiple checks.

The `if let Some` control flow is useful for handling the specific case where an `Option` holds a `Some` variant. It simplifies code and improves readability when working with the value contained in the `Some` variant.

Exercise

1. Enums and Complex Data: Design an enum to represent different types of geometric shapes (circle, square, triangle, etc.). Each enum variant should contain relevant data (radius, side length, etc.). Implement a function that calculates the area of each shape using pattern matching.

2. Implementing Methods: Extend the `String` type with a method that checks whether it's a palindrome. Test this method with various strings, including palindromes and non-palindromes.

Traits and Generics in Rust

In our earlier exploration of the `Result` and `Option` enums, you encountered using `<T, E>` and `<T>` within angle brackets. These constructs are known as generics. Generics are a powerful feature in programming that allows you to write functions, types, and structures that can work with different data types while maintaining type safety and code reusability.

Generics in Rust

Generics in Rust enable you to write code that can work with multiple data types without duplicating logic. This enhances code flexibility and maintainability by avoiding the need to write similar functions or structures for different types. The `T` and `E` placeholders you saw in `Result<T, E>` and `<T>` within `Option<T>` are examples of generic type parameters.

Using Generics in Functions

Let's start by looking at how generics are used in functions:

```rust
fn print_twice<T>(value: T) {
    println!("{:?}", value);
    println!("{:?}", value);
}

fn main() {
    print_twice(42);
    print_twice("Hello, Generics!");
}
```

In this example, print_twice takes a single argument value of type T, representing any data type. This function can work with both integers and strings without needing separate implementations. It can also work in any data type fed into it. Try this out.

Defining a Generic Struct

You can also define structs with generic fields:

```
// generic-typed struct with multiple types.
pub struct ExchangeTx<T, U> {
  pub amount: T,
  pub exchange_rate: U,
}

pub fn use_exchange_tx() {
  let dollar_to_transfer = ExchangeTx {
    amount: 500, exchange_rate: 940.80
  };

  println!("Your dollar value is {}, and the current exchange rate is {}", dollar_to_transfer.
amount, dollar_to_transfer.exchange_rate);
}
```

Here, ExchangeTx is a generic struct that can hold two values of potentially different types.

Implementing Traits with Generics

Traits are features that specify the functionalities available to a particular generic type. In programming languages like Go, traits are very similar to interfaces. A trait can be bound to a generic type to make it behave in a certain way.

Traits in Rust can also make use of generics. For example, the Display trait, which allows types to be formatted as strings, often uses generics:

```rust
use std::fmt::Display;

// Display Trait with Generics.
impl<T: Display, U:Display> ExchangeTx<T, U> {
    pub fn display_exchange_tx_info(&self) {
        let dollar_to_convert = ExchangeTx {
            amount: 500 as f64, exchange_rate: 940.85
        };

        println!("Your dollar value is {}, and the current exchange rate is {}", self.amount, self.exchange_rate);
    }
}

fn main() {
    // Create an instance of ExchangeTx.
    let exchange_tx = ExchangeTx {
        amount: 500 as f64,
        exchange_rate: 940.85,
    };

    // Call the method to display exchange transaction info.
    exchange_tx.display_exchange_tx_info();
}
```

In this case, the display_exchange_tx_info function takes any type that implements the Display trait as its argument. The Clone trait is another popularly used trait.

Constraints with Trait Bounds

You can place constraints on generic types using trait bounds to specify which traits the type must implement. This ensures that the generic code only works with types that meet those constraints:

```rust
fn show_display<T: Display>(item: T) {
    println!("{}", item);
}

fn main() {
    let string = "Hello, Generics!";
    show_display(string);

    let number = 42;
    // show_display(number); // Uncommenting this line will result in an error
}
```

We have been using the provided traits on our generic types. Let's create our custom trait and then see how to implement methods for generic types bounded by that trait.

For this example, let's consider a scenario where we're dealing with different types of databases in a backend system.

We'll create a trait called Database that defines methods for connecting to the database, querying, and saving data. Then, we'll implement this trait for two types of databases: SqlDatabase and NoSqlDatabase .

```rust
// Define a custom trait for different types of databases.
pub trait Database {
    fn connect(&self) -> bool;
    fn query(&self, query: &str) -> Vec<String>;
    fn save(&self, data: &str) -> bool;
}


// Implement the Database trait for an SQL database.
pub struct SqlDatabase {
    pub connection_string: String,
}
// Implement the generic trait's methods for the SqlDatabase type.
impl Database for SqlDatabase {
    fn connect(&self) -> bool {
        println!("Connected to SQL database: {}", self.connection_string);
        true
    }
    fn query(&self, query: &str) -> Vec<String> {
        println!("Executing SQL query: {}", query);
        vec!["Result 1".to_string(), "Result 2".to_string()]
    }
    fn save(&self, data: &str) -> bool {
        println!("Saving data to SQL database: {}", data);
        true
    }
}
```

```rust
// Implement the Database trait for a NoSQL database.
pub struct NoSqlDatabase {
  pub endpoint: String,
}

impl Database for NoSqlDatabase {
  fn connect(&self) -> bool {
    println!("Connected to NoSQL database: {}", self.endpoint);
    true
  }

  fn query(&self, query: &str) -> Vec<String> {
    println!("Executing NoSQL query: {}", query);
    vec!["Document 1".to_string(), "Document 2".to_string()]
  }

  fn save(&self, data: &str) -> bool {
    println!("Saving data to NoSQL database: {}", data);
    true
  }
}
```

```rust
fn main() {
    let sql_db = SqlDatabase {
        connection_string: "mysql://localhost:3306".to_string(),
    };

    sql_db.connect();
    sql_db.query("SELECT * FROM users");
    sql_db.save("New user data");

    let nosql_db = NoSqlDatabase {
        endpoint: "mongodb://localhost:27017".to_string(),
    };

    nosql_db.connect();
    nosql_db.query("db.collection.find()");
    nosql_db.save("New document");
}
```

In this example, we define a custom trait called Database with three methods: connect , query , and save . We then implement this trait for two different types of databases: SqlDatabase and NoSqlDatabase . Each implementation provides its logic for connecting, querying, and saving data. The main function demonstrates how you can use these implementations to interact with different databases.

Custom traits like Database allow you to define a common interface for different types, enabling polymorphism and code reuse in your backend system.

Note: If you put a pub keyword before a trait definition, you do not need to put it before the methods or functions that implement the trait. If you are writing the program inside a single main.rs file, you do not need pub anywhere.

Generics are a fundamental concept in Rust that enables you to write versatile, reusable, and type-safe code. They are particularly useful when creating functions, structs, or traits that can work with various data types while maintaining code efficiency and readability. Generics are a key tool for building flexible and maintainable code in Rust.

Lifetimes in Rust

Lifetimes are a fundamentally important concept in Rust that ensures that references remain valid and prevent issues like dangling pointers or references to memory that have been deallocated. To write safe and efficient Rust code, you must understand lifetimes and how to use them. This is one of Rust's most unique trademark features.

Lifetimes are annotations that specify how long references in your code are valid.

Lifetimes and function signatures

Before seeing an example, let's learn about some important concepts crucial to understanding lifetimes in Rust.

Managing References and Memory

Rust uses a strict borrowing model to manage memory and references. When you pass references around, the compiler ensures they're always valid and not used after the data they point to has been freed. This static checking, performed at compile time, prevents dangling pointers and helps you write safe and performant code.

Scope of Validity

Lifetimes let you define how long a reference is valid. This is particularly crucial when working with functions that accept or return references. Consider a scenario in your code where you calculate a hash for security purposes. To save memory and time, you want to pass references to the original data without copying it.

```
// without lifetimes.
fn calculate_hash(data: &Vec<u8>) -> Vec<u8> {
    // Calculate hash and return it
}
```

In this example, you're passing a reference to the data to avoid copying it, but there's no indication of how long this reference should be valid.

```
// with lifetimes.
fn calculate_hash<'a>(data: &'a Vec<u8>) -> Vec<u8> {
    // Calculate hash and return it
}
```

Let's see a more practical example with a simple program:

```
pub struct AllUser {
    pub id: u32,
    pub username: String,
}

impl AllUser {
    pub fn new(id: u32, username: String) -> Self {
        AllUser { id, username }
    }
}

pub fn find_longest_username(users: Vec<AllUser>) -> String {
    let mut longest_username = String::new();

    for user in users {
        if user.username.len() > longest_username.len() {
            longest_username = user.username;
        }
    }
    longest_username
}
```

```rust
fn main() {
  let users = vec![
    User::new(1, "alice".to_string()),
    User::new(2, "bob".to_string()),
    User::new(3, "charlie".to_string()),
  ];

  let longest_username = find_longest_username(users);
  println!("Longest username: {}", longest_username);
}
```

Now, with lifetimes:

```rust
pub struct LifetimeUsers<'a> {
  pub id: u32,
  pub username: &'a str,
}

impl<'a> LifetimeUsers<'a> {
  pub fn new(id: u32, username: &'a str) -> Self {
    LifetimeUsers {
      id,
      username
    }
  }
}
```

```rust
pub fn find_the_longest_username<'a>(users: Vec<LifetimeUsers<'a>>) -> &'a str {
    let mut longest_username = "";

    for user in users {
        if user.username.len() > longest_username.len() {
            longest_username = user.username;
        }
    }

    longest_username
}

fn main() {
    let users = vec![
        User::new(1, "alice"),
        User::new(2, "bob"),
        User::new(3, "charlie"),
    ];

    let longest_username = find_longest_username(users);
    println!("Longest username: {}", longest_username);
}
```

In the "Program Without Lifetimes" version, we work with owned String types for usernames. This requires cloning the username strings when creating User instances and updating the longest_username variable. This involves additional memory allocations and can be less efficient.

In the "Program With Lifetimes" version, we've changed the `User` struct to hold references to string slices (`&'a str`) for usernames. This means we're working with references to existing data instead of cloning. Lifetimes `'a` specify that the references in the `User` struct live as long as the `User` instances themselves.

Using lifetimes, we avoid unnecessary cloning and work with references guaranteed valid for their parent structs. This leads to more efficient memory usage and better performance.

That's a wrap concerning lifetimes. Let's learn something as important.

Advanced Functions and Closures

By now, you must be good at writing functions in Rust. If you have prior programming experience, you would know that functions sometimes accept pointers as parameters. If you know functional programming, you must have heard about higher-order functions and closures. Let's take them step by step.

Closures: syntax, capturing, and usage

Closures are anonymous functions that can capture variables from their surrounding scope. They are flexible and powerful tools for encapsulating behavior concisely.

Syntax

Here's a simple example of a closure that adds two numbers:

```
pub fn do_closure() {
  let add_closure = |x, y| x + y;
  let result = add_closure(10, 5);
  println!("Result: {}", result);
}

fn main() {
  // Use do_closure.
  do_closure();
}
```

Now, let's move on to Capturing.

Capturing

Closures can capture variables from their enclosing scope. They can capture variables by reference or by value. Consider this example:

```rust
pub fn do_capture() {
    let base = 10;
    let add_to_base = |x| x + base;
    let result = add_to_base(5);
    println!("Result: {}", result);
}

fn main() {
    // Use do_capture.
    do_capture();
}
```

The examples show how closures work in Rust: one or more variables are captured into an anonymous function denoted by pipes, the operation is carried out right after the capture, and the entire process is assigned to a variable. The variable can then be used as a function all along.

Let's see how this is done in a real system. We will use closures to customize the formatting of log messages based on their severity levels:

```rust
pub struct Logger {
    pub log_level: LogLevel,
}

pub enum LogLevel {
    Info,
    Warning,
    Error,
}

impl Logger {
    pub fn new(log_level: LogLevel) -> Self {
        Logger { log_level }
    }

    pub fn log(&self, message: &str, formatter: impl Fn(&str) -> String) {
        if self.should_log() {
            let formatted_message = formatter(message);
            println!("{}", formatted_message);

        }
    }
```

```rust
pub fn should_log(&self) -> bool {
    match self.log_level {
        LogLevel::Info => true,
        LogLevel::Warning => true,
        LogLevel::Error => true,
    }
  }
}

fn main() {
        let logger = Logger::new(LogLevel::Warning);
    let info_formatter = | message: &str | format!("INFO: {}", message);
    let warning_formatter = | message: &str | format!("WARNING: {}", message);
    let error_formatter = | message: &str | format!("ERROR: {}", message);

    logger.log("This is an information message", info_formatter);
    logger.log("This is a warning message", warning_formatter);
    logger.log("This is an error message", error_formatter);
}
```

In this example, we've defined a `Logger` struct with a `log` method that takes a message and a closure to format the message based on its severity level. The `Logger` struct also has a `should_log` method to determine whether a message should be logged based on the log level set during initialization.

We then define three formatting closures (`info_formatter`, `warning_formatter`, and `error_formatter`) that prepend the appropriate log level to the message.

In the `main` function, we create a `Logger` instance with a log level of `Warning`. We then log messages with different severity levels using the corresponding formatting closures. Since the log level is set to `Warning`, only the warning and error messages are logged.

This example showcases how closures can encapsulate behavior and customize functionality. In a backend scenario, you could extend this logging system to include additional features such as writing logs to files, sending logs to remote servers, or integrating with third-party logging libraries.

Function Pointers and Higher-Order Functions

Rust supports functional programming. Thus, you can write functions to receive anything as value, including other functions, and to return anything as a result, including other functions. This opens the door to using function pointers and higher-order functions.

Function pointers

A function pointer refers to the memory location of a function. They're useful for scenarios where you want to pass functions as arguments or store them in data structures. Here's a basic example:

```
pub fn add(x: i32, y: i32) -> i32 {
  x + y
}

pub fn subtract(x: i32, y: i32) -> i32 {
  x - y
}

pub fn calculate(operation: fn(i32, i32) -> i32, x: i32, y: i32) -> i32 {
  operation(x, y)
}
```

The identity of the function pointer is not known at compile time.

Higher-Order functions

These are functions that take other functions as arguments or return functions. They allow you to create more abstract and reusable code. Consider the following example that implements a higher-order function for applying a function to each element of a vector:

```rust
pub fn apply_operation(operation: fn(i32) -> i32, number: i32) -> i32 {
    operation(number)
}

pub fn square(x: i32) -> i32 {
    x * x
}

pub fn double(x: i32) -> i32 {
    x * 2
}

fn main() {
    let num = 5;
    let squared_result = apply_operation(square, num);
    println!("Square of {} is {}.", num, squared_result);

    let doubled_result = apply_operation(double, num);
    println!("Double of {} is {}.", num, doubled_result);
}
```

Using a real-world example, let's see how higher-order functions that have closures are written. Below, we simulate a data processing pipeline for user data:

```rust
pub struct User {
    pub id: u32,
    pub name: String,
    pub age: u32,
}

fn main() {
        // Higher-order functions with closures.
    let hof_users = vec![
        advanced::hof::User { id: 1, name: "Alice".to_string(), age: 18 },
        advanced::hof::User { id: 2, name: "Bob".to_string(), age: 32 },
        advanced::hof::User { id: 3, name: "Charlie".to_string(), age: 24 },
    ];

    // Higher-order function: map
    let names: Vec<String> = hof_users.iter().map(|user| user.name.clone()).collect();
    println!("User names: {:?}", names);

    // Higher-order function: filter
    let adults: Vec<&User> = hof_users.iter().filter(|user| user.age >= 18).collect();
    println!("Adult users: {:?}", adults);

    // Higher-order function: reduce (fold)
    let total_age: u32 = hof_users.iter().map(|user| user.age).fold(0, |acc, age| acc + age);
    println!("Total age of all users: {}", total_age);
}
```

In this example, we have a User struct representing user data. Our goal is to use higher-order functions to process this data differently.

Map

We start by using the map higher-order function to transform the user data. We create a new vector containing only the names of the users using the map function and a closure that extracts the name field from each user.

This demonstrates how higher-order functions can transform data into a different format.

Filter

Next, we use the filter higher-order function to select specific users based on a condition. We create a new vector containing only the adult users (those aged 18 or older) using the filter function and a closure that checks the age field. This showcases how higher-order functions can be used for data filtering.

Reduce (Fold)

Finally, we utilize the fold higher-order function to perform a reduction operation on the user data. We calculate the total age of all users using the fold function and a closure that accumulates the ages. This demonstrates how higher-order functions can be used for data aggregation.

Exercise

1. Higher-Order Functions: Write a higher-order function that takes a vector of integers and returns a new vector containing only the even numbers.

2. Closures: Create a program that simulates an online auction. Implement a bidding mechanism using closures to define the behavior of placing bids and determining the winner.

Concurrency and Multithreading in Rust

This chapter will explore the world of concurrency and multithreading in Rust. Concurrency allows you to handle multiple tasks simultaneously, while multithreading takes advantage of multiple CPU cores for parallel execution. Rust's strong ownership and type system help ensure safe and efficient concurrent programming.

Introduction to Concurrency and Parallelism

Concurrency is the concept of executing multiple tasks seemingly simultaneously. It's crucial for efficiently utilizing system resources and building responsive applications. Parallelism takes concurrency further by executing tasks simultaneously using multiple threads or processes.

Rust's ownership system and memory safety make it a robust choice for concurrent programming. The Rust compiler enforces strict rules that prevent data races and memory access issues, ensuring safer multithreaded code.

Using Rust's std::thread for Multithreading

Rust provides a powerful threading library, std::thread, for creating and managing threads. Threads allow different parts of your program to execute independently and in parallel. Here's a basic example of using threads to perform tasks concurrently:

```rust
use std::thread;

fn main() {
  let handle1 = thread::spawn(|| {
    for i in 1..=5 {
      println!("Thread 1: {}", i);
    }
  });

  let handle2 = thread::spawn(|| {
    for i in 1..=5 {
      println!("Thread 2: {}", i);
    }
  });

  handle1.join().unwrap();
  handle2.join().unwrap();

  println!("Main thread completed.");
}
```

In this example, two threads are spawned to print numbers concurrently. The `join` method ensures that the main thread waits for these spawned threads to complete before continuing.

Safely Sharing Data between Threads with std::sync

When multiple threads share data, the potential for data races arises, leading to unpredictable behavior. Rust addresses this issue with its ownership model and the `std::sync` module, which provides synchronization primitives for safe data sharing.

The `Arc` (atomic reference counter) and `Mutex` (mutual exclusion) are commonly used to share data safely between threads:

```rust
use std::sync::{Arc, Mutex};
use std::thread;

fn main() {
    let counter = Arc::new(Mutex::new(0));
    let mut handles = vec![];

    for _ in 0..10 {
        let counter_clone = Arc::clone(&counter);
        let handle = thread::spawn(move || {
            let mut value = counter_clone.lock().unwrap();
            *value += 1;
        });
        handles.push(handle);
    }

    for handle in handles {
        handle.join().unwrap();
    }

    println!("Final counter value: {:?}", *counter.lock().unwrap());
}
```

In this example, the `Arc` ensures reference counting across threads, and the `Mutex` ensures exclusive access to the data, avoiding data races. Threads increment a counter concurrently, and we safely print the final counter value at the end.

Rust's concurrency and multithreading are worth a deeper look, and learning just the basics here won't suffice when you need to write concurrent code.

Error Handling in Rust

Errors occur in software development, and Rust provides a wonderful set of features for handling errors.

In this chapter, we'll delve into Rust's intricacies of error handling. Effective error handling is a cornerstone of robust and reliable software. We'll explore the Result and Option types, learn how to use the match and ? operators for error handling, implement custom error types using the thiserror crate, and discover how the Result type aids in early returns within functions. This chapter will use real-world backend engineering scenarios to illustrate each concept.

Dealing with Errors Using Result and Option

In Rust, errors are handled through the Result and Option enums. Result represents a computation that might fail and returns either an Ok value containing the result or an Err value containing an error. Conversely, an Option is used when a value could be present (Some) or absent (None).

Consider an example of opening a file, a common operation in backend systems:

```
use std::fs::File;

fn open_file(path: &str) -> Result<File, std::io::Error> {
    let file = File::open(path)?;
    Ok(file)
}

fn main() {
    let file_result = open_file("example.txt");
    match file_result {
        Ok(file) => println!("File opened successfully: {:?}", file),
        Err(err) => println!("Error opening file: {}", err),
    }
}
```

In this example, the `open_file` function returns a `Result<File, std::io::Error>`. We use the `?` operator to propagate errors and handle them gracefully using pattern matching.

Using `match` and `?` for Error Handling

The `match` statement is a powerful tool for handling different error scenarios. It allows you to pattern match against different error types and take appropriate actions.

Continuing from the previous example, let's illustrate using `match` and `?` to read from the opened file:

```
use std::io::Read;

fn read_file(file: &mut File) -> Result<String, std::io::Error> {
  let mut content = String::new();
  file.read_to_string(&mut content)?;
  Ok(content)
}

fn main() {
  let file_result = open_file("example.txt");
  match file_result {
    Ok(mut file) => {
      let content_result = read_file(&mut file);
      match content_result {
        Ok(content) => println!("File content:\\\\n{}", content),
        Err(err) => println!("Error reading file content: {}", err),
      }
    }
    Err(err) => println!("Error opening file: {}", err),
  }
}
```

The nested match statements handle both opening the file and reading its content, ensuring proper error handling at each step.

Implementing Custom Error Types with thiserror Crate

Rust allows you to define your error types for better code organization and expressiveness. The thiserror crate simplifies the process of creating custom error types.

Consider a scenario where you're building a backend system that interacts with a database:

```rust
use thiserror::Error;
use rusqlite::Error as SqliteError;

#[derive(Error, Debug)]
enum DatabaseError {
  #[error("SQL error: {0}")]
  Sql(#[from] SqliteError),
  #[error("Connection error: {0}")]
  Connection(String),
  #[error("Query execution failed")]
  QueryFailed,
}

fn execute_query() -> Result<(), DatabaseError> {
  // ... code to execute a query
  Err(DatabaseError::QueryFailed)
}

fn main() {
  if let Err(err) = execute_query() {
    match err {
      DatabaseError::Sql(sql_err) => println!("SQL error: {}", sql_err),
      DatabaseError::Connection(msg) => println!("Connection error: {}", msg),
      DatabaseError::QueryFailed => println!("Query execution failed"),
    }
  }
}
```

In this example, we define a custom DatabaseError enum using the thiserror crate. We create variants for different types of database errors, and the #[from] attribute allows us to convert other error types (e.g., SqliteError) into our custom error type.

Using Result for Early Returns in Functions

Rust encourages the use of the Result type for early returns in functions. This approach ensures that errors are handled gracefully without complex nesting.

Imagine a backend service that processes user payments:

```rust
struct Payment {
    amount: f64,
}

fn process_payment(payment: Payment) -> Result<(), String> {
    if payment.amount <= 0.0 {
        return Err("Invalid payment amount".to_string());
    }

    // ... process the payment

    Ok(())
}

fn main() {
    let payment = Payment { amount: 100.0 };
    if let Err(err) = process_payment(payment) {
        println!("Error processing payment: {}", err);
    } else {
        println!("Payment processed successfully");
    }
}
```

In this example, the process_payment function uses Result to handle both success and error cases. By returning Err early if the payment amount is invalid, we avoid unnecessary computation and ensure clear error handling.

Error handling is a critical aspect of writing reliable backend systems. Rust's `Result` and `Option` types, combined with the `match` and `?` operators, provide robust mechanisms for dealing with errors concisely and safely. Additionally, custom error types and libraries like `thiserror` enable you to create expressive and organized error handling code.

Using the `Result` type for early returns makes your functions more readable and maintainable. The next chapter will focus on file I/O and serialization, essential for handling data in software applications.

Exercise

1. Custom Error Types: Modify the task manager application to include error handling using custom error types. Define error variants for various scenarios, such as invalid input, file read/write errors, etc.

2. thiserror Crate: Refactor your custom error types to utilize the `thiserror` crate for more concise and structured error handling. Experiment with adding context and additional information to your error messages.

File I/O and Serialization

This comprehensive chapter will explore Rust's file input/output (I/O) operations and serialization. These topics are crucial for handling data in backend applications. We'll explore how to read and write files, perform serialization and deserialization using the `serde` crate, and work with various file formats like JSON and YAML. This chapter will use practical examples from a backend engineering perspective.

Reading and Writing Files in Rust

File I/O is a fundamental operation in many backend systems. Rust provides a robust standard library for handling file operations. Let's consider a scenario where we need to read from and write to a configuration file:

```rust
use std::fs::{File, OpenOptions};
use std::io::{Read, Write};

fn read_config_file(file_path: &str) -> Result<String, std::io::Error> {
    let mut content = String::new();
    let mut file = File::open(file_path)?;
    file.read_to_string(&mut content)?;
    Ok(content)
}

fn write_config_file(file_path: &str, content: &str) -> Result<(), std::io::Error> {
    let mut file = OpenOptions::new()
        .write(true)
        .create(true)
        .truncate(true)
        .open(file_path)?;
    file.write_all(content.as_bytes())?;
    Ok(())
}
```

```rust
fn main() {
    let file_path = "config.txt";
    let config_content = read_config_file(file_path);
    match config_content {
        Ok(content) => println!("Config content: {}", content),
        Err(err) => println!("Error reading config file: {}", err),
    }

    let new_config_content = "new config content";
    if let Err(err) = write_config_file(file_path, new_config_content) {
        println!("Error writing config file: {}", err);
    } else {
        println!("Config file updated successfully");
    }
}
```

In this example, the read_config_file function reads content from a file, and the write_config_file function writes content to a file. Both functions return a Result to handle potential errors.

Serialization and Deserialization using serde

Serialization and deserialization are essential for converting structured data into a format that can be stored or transmitted and reconstructed. The serde crate simplifies this process.

Consider a scenario where we're dealing with user profiles:

```rust
use serde::{Serialize, Deserialize};
use std::fs;

#[derive(Serialize, Deserialize, Debug)]
struct UserProfile {
    id: u32,
    username: String,
    email: String,
}

fn main() {
    let user = UserProfile {
        id: 1,
        username: "alice".to_string(),
        email: "test@test.com".to_string(),
    };

    // Serialization to JSON
    let json_data = serde_json::to_string(&user).unwrap();
    println!("Serialized JSON: {}", json_data);

    // Deserialization from JSON
    let deserialized_user: UserProfile = serde_json::from_str(&json_data).unwrap();
    println!("Deserialized User: {:?}", deserialized_user);
}
```

64

In this example, the UserProfile struct implements the Serialize and Deserialize traits from serde . We use the serde_json module to serialize the user data into JSON format and then deserialize it.

Working with Different File Formats

Backend systems often need to work with various file formats. Let's take an example where we're dealing with YAML configuration files:

```rust
use serde::{Serialize, Deserialize};
use std::fs;

#[derive(Serialize, Deserialize, Debug)]
struct AppConfig {
  server_address: String,
  port: u16,
}

fn read_yaml_config(file_path: &str) -> Result<AppConfig, serde_yaml::Error> {
  let content = fs::read_to_string(file_path)?;
  let config: AppConfig = serde_yaml::from_str(&content)?;
  Ok(config)
}

fn main() {
  let file_path = "config.yaml";
  let config_result = read_yaml_config(file_path);
  match config_result {
    Ok(config) => println!("Server address: {}, Port: {}", config.server_address, config.port),
    Err(err) => println!("Error reading YAML config: {}", err),
  }
}
```

In this example, we use the `serde_yaml` module to handle YAML serialization and deserialization. The `read_yaml_config` function reads the YAML configuration file and returns the parsed `AppConfig` struct.

File I/O and serialization are pivotal in backend engineering for managing data and configuring applications. Rust's standard library provides robust tools for reading and writing files, while the `serde` crate simplifies serialization and deserialization. You can seamlessly integrate data into your backend systems using various file formats like JSON and YAML. In the final chapter, we'll build upon these concepts and embark on a milestone project to reinforce your understanding of Rust in real-world scenarios.

Exercise

1. JSON to Struct: Create a JSON file containing information about multiple books. Write a program that reads the JSON file, parses its contents, and converts them into a vector of custom `Book` structs. Display the information in these books.

2. YAML Serialization: Modify the task manager application to save tasks as YAML files instead of JSON. Implement serialization and deserialization using the `serde_yaml` crate. Test the application's ability to read and write tasks in YAML format.

3. Explore Serialization and Deserialization in Rust.

Building a Task Management App

We'll build a task management application using Rust in this exciting milestone project. This project will encompass concepts covered in the previous chapters, including structuring your code, error handling, file I/O, and more. Following these steps, you'll create a functional task manager allowing users to add, list, and mark tasks as completed.

Note: The complete implementation is done at the end, but you are given free rein to use your newly acquired knowledge to implement the functions.

Step 1: Project Setup

1. Create a new Rust project using Cargo:

```
cargo new task_manager
```

2. Navigate to the project directory:

```
cd task_manager
```

Step 2: Define Task Struct

1. Open the src/main.rs file and define a Task struct:

```
struct Task {
    id: u32,
    title: String,
    completed: bool,
}
```

Step 3: Implement Basic Functions

1. Inside the `main` function, create an empty vector to store tasks:

```rust
fn main() {
    let mut tasks: Vec<Task> = Vec::new();
    // ...
}
```

2. Implement a function to add tasks:

```rust
fn add_task(tasks: &mut Vec<Task>, title: &str) {
    let id = (tasks.len() + 1) as u32;
    let task = Task { id, title: title.to_string(), completed: false };
    tasks.push(task);
}
```

3. Implement a function to list tasks:

```rust
fn list_tasks(tasks: &[Task]) {
    for task in tasks {
        let status = if task.completed { "[X]" } else { "[ ]" };
        println!("{} {}: {}", status, task.id, task.title);
    }
}
```

4. Implement a function to mark tasks as completed:

```rust
fn complete_task(tasks: &mut Vec<Task>, id: u32) -> Result<(), String> {
    if let Some(task) = tasks.iter_mut().find(|t| t.id == id) {
        task.completed = true;
        Ok(())
    } else {
        Err("Task not found".to_string())
    }
}
```

Step 4: Implement File I/O

1. Create a tasks.txt file in the project directory with task data.

2. Implement a function to read tasks from the file:

```rust
fn read_tasks_from_file(file_path: &str) -> Result<Vec<Task>, std::io::Error> {
    // Read tasks from the file and return them as a Vec<Task>
}
```

3. Implement a function to write tasks to the file:

```rust
fn write_tasks_to_file(file_path: &str, tasks: &[Task]) -> Result<(), std::io::Error> {
    // Write tasks to the file
}
```

Step 5: Integrate Error Handling

1. Update functions to return Result with custom error types.

2. Implement the main function:

```rust
fn main() -> Result<(), Box<dyn std::error::Error>> {
    // Load tasks from the file
    let tasks = read_tasks_from_file("tasks.txt")?;

    // ...

    // Save tasks to the file
    write_tasks_to_file("tasks.txt", &tasks)?;

    Ok(())
}
```

Step 6: User Interaction

1. Implement a simple command-line interface using the stdin module to handle user input.

2. Parse user commands to add, list, and mark tasks as completed.

Step 7: Run and Test

1. Run the project using Cargo:

```
cargo run
```

2. Test your task manager by adding, listing, and completing tasks using the command-line interface.

Step 8: Enhancements

1. Consider enhancing the project by adding more features like editing, deleting, and prioritizing tasks.

2. Explore additional Rust libraries, like colored terminal output or interactive input libraries, to improve the user experience.

Congratulations! You've successfully built a task management application using Rust. This milestone project combines concepts learned throughout the tutorial to create a practical and functional application. Keep exploring Rust and applying these concepts to more ambitious projects.

Appendix

Here's the complete code for the task management application, as described in the milestone project:

```rust
use std::fs;
use std::io::{Read, Write};
use std::env;
use serde_json

struct Task {
    id: u32,
    title: String,
    completed: bool,
}

fn add_task(tasks: &mut Vec<Task>, title: &str) {
    let id = (tasks.len() + 1) as u32;
    let task = Task {
        id,
        title: title.to_string(),
        completed: false,
    };
    tasks.push(task);
}
```

```rust
fn list_tasks(tasks: &[Task]) {
    for task in tasks {
        let status = if task.completed { "[X]" } else { "[ ]" };
        println!("{} {}: {}", status, task.id, task.title);
    }
}

fn complete_task(tasks: &mut Vec<Task>, id: u32) -> Result<(), String> {
    if let Some(task) = tasks.iter_mut().find(|t| t.id == id) {
        task.completed = true;
        Ok(())
    } else {
        Err("Task not found".to_string())
    }
}
```

```rust
fn read_tasks_from_file(file_path: &str) -> Result<Vec<Task>, std::io::Error> {
    let mut content = String::new();
    let mut file = fs::File::open(file_path)?;
    file.read_to_string(&mut content)?;

    let tasks: Vec<Task> = serde_json::from_str(&content)?;
    Ok(tasks)
}

fn write_tasks_to_file(file_path: &str, tasks: &[Task]) -> Result<(), std::io::Error> {
    let json_data = serde_json::to_string(tasks)?;
    let mut file = fs::File::create(file_path)?;
    file.write_all(json_data.as_bytes())?;
    Ok(())
}
```

```rust
fn main() -> Result<(), Box<dyn std::error::Error>> {
    let args: Vec<String> = env::args().collect();
    let file_path = "tasks.txt";

    let mut tasks = if fs::metadata(file_path).is_ok() {
        read_tasks_from_file(file_path)?
    } else {
        Vec::new()
    };

    ...
```

```rust
match args.get(1).map(|arg| arg.as_str()) {
    Some("add") => {
        let title = args.get(2).ok_or("Title not provided")?;
        add_task(&mut tasks, title);
    }
    Some("list") => {
        list_tasks(&tasks);
    }
    Some("complete") => {
        let id = args
            .get(2)
            .ok_or("Task ID not provided")?
            .parse::<u32>()
            .map_err(|_| "Invalid task ID")?;
        complete_task(&mut tasks, id)?;
    }
    _ => {
        println!("Usage:");
        println!("task_manager add <title>");
        println!("task_manager list");
        println!("task_manager complete <task_id>");
    }
}
write_tasks_to_file(file_path, &tasks)?;

Ok(())
}
```

To run this code, follow these steps:

1. Install the serde and serde_json crates by adding the following dependencies to your Cargo.toml file:

```
[dependencies]
serde = "1.0"
serde_json = "1.0"
```

1. Save the above code to the src/main.rs file within your task_manager project directory.

2. Run the project using Cargo:

```
cargo run add "Buy groceries"
cargo run add "Complete project"
cargo run list
cargo run complete 1
```

This code demonstrates the complete task management application, including file I/O, error handling, and user interaction. Adjust the code as needed and explore enhancements to make the application more robust and user-friendly.

Want more?

Get Advanced Rust

What you will learn:

1. Advanced Ownership:
2. Unsafe Rust:
3. Advanced Patterns and Idioms:
4. Meta-programming with Macros
5. FFI and Interoperability
6. Performance and Optimization
7. Milestone Project: Web Server in Rust
8. Exercise to improve your Rust skills

Grab Your Copy Now

https://masteringbackend.com/books/advanced-rust